Table of Contents

Lesson 1: List Building for New Marketers......... 2

```
Introduction..................................................  3
Public & Private JV Gateways.....................  6
Solo Ads......................................................  8
Ad Swaps....................................................  10
Click Banking..............................................  12
Free WSOs...................................................  13
PPV/CPV List Building................................  15
Bartering for Leads.....................................  17
Your Own Affiliate Program........................  19
Exit Popups.................................................  21
Reverse opt-in Form...................................  23
Buying Ad space direct from webmasters.  24
Nested Squeeze Page on Blog...................  26
Tell-A-Friend Script....................................  28
Integrated Cross-Promotions.....................  29
Viral PDF Reports.......................................  30
Affiliate list Cross-Promotions...................  31
```

Lesson 2: Niche Marketing Resource Guide........... 32

```
Part 1: Getting Niche Ideas.....................  33
Part 2: Pruning Your List of Niches.........  41
```

Lesson 3: Paid Traffic Bargain hunters................. 50

```
Introduction..............................................  51
Advertising Sources..................................  52-62
```

Copyright © 2018 Taylor NTerprise LLC

Lesson 1
List Building
For New Marketers

by Kevin Taylor

Copyright © 2018 Taylor NTerprise LLC

Introduction

What you're about to get is a combination of new and old list building tactics that I've gathered since 2008 up until now in 2018.

Just to be clear... I'm going to only share what's working RIGHT NOW.

When I go over the older tactics I'm going to talk about how well they work RIGHT NOW and how I'm using them TODAY.

What I'm going to share with you is not just the tactics themselves, but some I'm going to point out to you and tell you which ones have built me the most subscribers, for example, and which ones are working the best for me right now.

I don't want you to look at this as if it's a written report, I want you to look at it as if it's lifechanging knowledge and information because it doesn't matter if it's written on a napkin.

It doesn't matter if it's on audio.

It doesn't matter if it's on video.

It doesn't matter if it's in a PDF.

It doesn't even matter if someone is teaching it to you one-on-one over the phone or one-on-one through a webinar or through group coaching; it's all information, and this powerful information is the most powerful information that I've ever come across online.

List building has been the key to my success over the years and I have a lot of people to thank for that, but I mostly have to thank myself because I've gone out of my way to explore all of these realms of list building.

Copyright © 2018 Taylor NTerprise LLC

The first thing you need to know is that business and making sales depends on fresh lead flow.

What I mean is you want constant leads coming in.

If I were you, I would start aiming to generate something like 250 subscribers per day.

You might be thinking, that's a lot of subscribers, or it's going to be too expensive.

Well, there are great paid lead sources; there are also very good free ones that you can use to build up your list to generate 250 or more subscribers per day.

Once you hit 250 subscribers per day or more, then it's all a matter of focusing on converting them and then just doing the list building stuff you're doing over and over and over and getting the same results all the time.

Converting them is another thing and this report isn't going to be anything at all about converting leads into sales, it's all about generating lead flow.

As I was telling you, I can't stress this enough that the bulk of your money that you make is going to come from the people who are the newest on your list.

The older a lead gets, the less responsive they become, generally, especially if you're an affiliate.

Now if you're a product creator and you do classes and such, you may find that some of your older subscribers are the most profitable subscribers you have because they're your own customers who enroll in all of your classes; all of your $1,000 classes and whatnot.

As an affiliate, it's different; you don't have that retention.

See, when you're a product creator, it's easier to keep the retention of your list.

I've found this to be true. That's one of the reasons why I'm starting to create more and more products now, although over the years I've been mainly just an affiliate.

Copyright © 2018 Taylor NTerprise LLC

If you are just an affiliate, again, your normal focus should be fresh leads and keeping your leads coming in on a daily basis.

That's at least 250 leads a day.

If you're a product creator, you may not need as high of a lead flow, but why not do both?

Why not be a creator that keeps retouching the list and also generate 250 subscribers or more to your list?

Let's go ahead and get into this because I have tons and tons of list building methods and strategies to cover for you now.

Public and Private JV Giveaways

The first one is JV giveaways.

JV giveaways haven't changed much as far as public JV giveaways go.

You can go to newjvgiveaways.com anytime you want and jump in on any JV giveaways.

But what has surfaced since 2011 is something called the private giveaway.

There are a lot of little private giveaways taking place that you can be part of all over the internet.

You can go to people who are just as big as you are online, and even bigger, and start a private JV giveaway with them.

What I mean is you can get 5 to 10 or more people in on a private giveaway, where no one else can join and be a contributor.

This means that the people who are on there, who are contributors, are responsible for generating all the traffic to the giveaway and there is a WordPress plug-in that you can use to host your own private giveaways called WP Venture.

Now go do a search on Google for WP Venture and it's being sold on the Warrior Forum for chump change, as a Warrior Special Offer.

A giveaway is where a group of contributors come together and will submit their gifts.

People who come and join the giveaway as members are going to opt in to different giveaways and this will add subscribers to your list.

If you've been around for a while, you no doubt know what JV giveaways are, and I'm not going to dwell on what JV giveaways are or how they can build good business for you because you can go to a place like newjvgiveaways.com and find out all you need to know about giveaways freely on the net.

But just the fact that I'm pointing you in that direction is pretty valuable because if you're just starting out and you have no money to spend on ads, getting giveaways is a really good way to start, because you can add that first 10, 50, 100 subscribers on your list fairly quickly.

Some of these giveaways get up to 30,000 subscribers joining; not to your list, but to the actual giveaway. What happens is the host of the giveaway is going to get the most subscribers.

They're putting the giveaway with all the contributors and setting the dates, and then once the giveaway is live, all the contributors send traffic to the JV giveaway main page, but the host is going to get all the subscribers onto their list. Then the member who just joined will probably see a one-time offer or some kind of offer before they go and see all the different gifts that that contributors have. When you're a contributor and you promote one of these JV giveaways through your own link, you often make sales right there before they even get to the gifts. That's one thing about it.

If you're just starting out and you don't have much money to buy traffic, then this may be one that you want to master. The truth is, if you became just a master of one of these methods, then you'll generate all the ads you'll ever need.

Let me say that again.

If you become the master of just one of these methods I'm going to share with you then you will generate all the leads you'll ever need. So why not do something like JV giveaways? You can do public ones, you can do private ones, and you can host ones and make the real money. I've hosted a couple and that's where I generated the most leads. You could generate 10,000 leads in one day, 20,000 leads in one day from contributors blasting traffic to your own giveaway.

Just think about that. If you were to jump headfirst into the world of JV giveaways as a contributor to start off with, then one day you may be able to host your own JV giveaways.

Solo Ads

The next list building tactic I want to talk about is solo ads.

When I'm actively running solo ads, I'm usually able to generate hundreds of leads per day, right now, this year. This may change down the road, but as of right now, this year, solo ads are cheap, they're effective and very easy. Because of this, you don't have to worry about landing page quality score or paying per click and keeping an eye on your ad's ad paying by the click.

What you're getting is an ad that goes out to a subscriber list, so whenever you buy a solo ad; let's say you buy a solo ad for $300 for 1,000 clicks to your site, you pay 30 cents per click to your site and you know exactly how many clicks are going to come to your site and the guy who sends you a solo ad sends an ad out to his email list, which recommends your freebie or your website. They're transferring their authority over to you, in a way, that's what makes it the most effective way of generating traffic right now, in my opinion. Because the ads are still cheap, it's very effective for anybody who has the money to risk on it.

One place you can find a lot of great solo ad deals is by getting on Skype and talking to different solo ad sellers. I realize it's not going to be easy just to find a solo ad seller, or any solo ad sellers if you have no clue about the world of solo ads right now, but once you find some solo ad sellers, you want to start connecting with them on Skype and getting into the world of solo ads because you can meet so many different solo ad sellers who will give you great deals on Skype that they don't give outside of Skype.

You can find solo ads at one place called soloaddirectory.com. That's where I would go if I were going to go and look for solo ads right now. The key to have profitable solo ads is your sales funnel. You want to have the squeeze page that generates the free leads that gives away something. Then you have an upsell from there, which will be a one-time offer for something that's below the $17 price point and then you want to have up-sells from there so you can afford to pay for your solo ads.

Now, you may also want to promote things on the download page for your freebies that you're giving away. That way you can come close to breaking even or you can profit directly right away from that solo ad before you even get the subscribers on your list. Although many solo ads I haven't profited from right up front, I made a profit on the backend from promoting strictly to the subscriber list.

That's something you have to think about.

A lot of companies in advertising are willing to pay a lot of money upfront and even lose money on the front end because they know they're going to make money on the backend with their follow up marketing, which is what email marketing is all about.

Ad Swaps

Ad swaps are where you send out an ad to your list promoting someone else's squeeze page and then someone else does the same for you to their list. It's similar to solo ads except for no one is buying anything; you're just trading off ads.

The place where everybody has moved to these days is called safe-swaps.com.

There used to be a site called IMadswaps.com, which was like an ad swap forum.

There are other forums that kind of emerged in the last few years and they've pretty much slowed down because of safe-swaps.com. The thing about ad swaps is that it is getting less effective because seeing that it emerged around 2009, that's when everyone was discovering ad swaps and starting to do it. Now people are over-mailing their lists with ad swaps. They're doing way more ad swaps so they're getting less responses from the subscribers. Retention rates are going down, click thru rates are going down. But, if you still want to generate hundreds of leads per day, you still can do that.

The key to profiting from ad swaps is the same key to profiting with solo ads, which is your sales funnel. If you've got a good sales funnel, you can use it for your ad swaps. Also, ad swaps are a great way to test your sales funnel before you start buying something like solo ads.

You're probably going to get less quality leads from ad swaps than you are solo ads, yet it's still a good indication of whether your sales funnel will convert traffic into sales, and that's what's necessary to profit with ad swaps, because you're not promoting anything that's going to be making money directly to your list; you're promoting someone else's squeeze page, so you're relying on the traffic coming from the JV partner's list to your sales funnel. Depending on your sales funnel, you can do ad swaps every single day if you want to, become the master of ad swaps and just tweak your sales funnel and have very good business there.

You don't want to overcomplicate marketing. This kind of thinking is really profitable if you could get super focused. Think about how simple this business is right here.

You put together a sales funnel.

You do ad swaps every day.

You test your sales funnel every day until you're converting the maximum amount of visitors who land on your page.
That in itself is a business no matter what anyone says. That's what I try to do in my business... SIMPLIFY.

I have a daily routine that I try to simplify down more and more every day until that is just brain dead stupid, and lately, it has been solo ads because I've found that I'm getting the best returns on solo ads. But if I didn't have any money, I would start off with JV giveaways just to generate 100 subscribers or so, then I would move to safe-swaps.com and I would start ad swapping. That's what I would do if I didn't have any money.

Click Banking

There's also another thing I would want to do if I didn't have any money and I had a small list. This goes out to the small list owners, people who are just starting their lists and what not. If you have a list of 100 people or 1,000 people, you could start doing what's called click banking. It has nothing to do with ClickBank.com but what it is, is you go to a marketer with a huge list and you say, "I will send you 100 clicks or 1,000 clicks over the course of this month (clicks mean visitors) and what you will do is return those clicks all at once after I'm done."

What happens is the big marketer with a big list will give you a tracking link to use on all your emails. You'll work hard to build up your traffic to them through that link, and then when you're ready to cash in your clicks you go to them and say, "I'd like to cash in my clicks," and then they send you clicks; they send you as many as you have sent them. This is really similar to ad swaps, as you can see, but it works out well for small list owners because you can just focus on sending traffic to one big marketer without having to set up all kinds of ad swap deals. For example, if you have an email follow up series, the first couple of days of your email follow up series could be sending the new people on your list to another marketer who you are click banking with. This isn't the greatest advice for product creators.

I don't think that ad swaps or click banking is a great idea for product creators because if you're a product creator, then you can have so much longevity on your own list by just promoting your own products.

If you're a product creator, you might want to just focus on paid methods and getting affiliates to promote your stuff, but that's just my opinion and that's what I've seen from experience.

As an affiliate marketer, who doesn't have a ton of products to promote to the list all month, who doesn't crank out many products, it's all about fresh lead flow, like I was saying in the beginning of this report.

Things like ad swaps and click banking are the mother-load of free, fresh lead flow.

Copyright © 2018 Taylor NTerprise LLC

Free WSOs

Let's get into another method, which is something I've been doing since 2008 or so, which is running free WSO's.

I'm talking about freebies that I give away on the Warrior Forum, which is WarriorForum.com and WSO stands for Warrior Special Offers.

They will give away products on the Warrior Special Offers forum in exchange for opt-ins.

One thing that I've noticed between the Warrior Forum and the leads you may get from ad swaps, click banking, and solo ads, is that Warrior Forum traffic is used to buying lower priced products. Your funnel may be a lot different for free WSO's than it will be with ad swaps, click banking, or solo ads.

For one of my funnels they get a freebie on the squeeze page, then the OTO after that is a $10 offer, then the OTO after that is another $10 offer. You can see I'm keeping it at $10 or less because I know they buy $10 or less things, whereas with ad swaps, click banking, and solo ads I'll have a freebie, a $9 offer, then to a $97 OTO and then it will go up from there.
Good luck trying to sell a $97 to Warrior Forum members because it's not going to happen, unless you have a done-4-u service or something that's worth 25x $97 price points. It's just a different world there, but the good thing about running free WSO's is that's a business in itself, if you want it to be because you can run free WSO's and then you can promote WSO's as an affiliate to promote programs like offers through WSO Pro, which is at WarriorPlus.com or JVzoo.com or DigiResults.com.

Do you remember how I was talking about in one of the other sections how you can make a business just by focusing on one thing? Well, this is a business for you too.

Think about this.

This is all you need to do is to run free WSO's. You can have six or seven free WSO's for six or seven different freebies that you create and you can rotate those once a day so that you're launching a new WSO a day, but it's giving away one of your six or seven freebies. You can generate your list like that and your sales funnel will get you close to breaking even or making a profit right away on the front end, then on the backend you can promote WSO's as an affiliate to your list you've built.

I've been known to have multiple free WSO's that I rotate on a daily basis and I've done that model before. If you get bored with certain things in marketing, then try different models.

I just simplify things and just go at them with a very narrow focus.

Right now, I might be buying a lot of solo ads and doing what I described in the Solo Ads section, but just months ago, I was buying a lot of free WSO's and trying to get as many leads as I could with that and just promoting WSO's every day and making plenty of money.

Once you get that, narrow focus and simplify everything, everything becomes clear and you can make a lot of money just focusing on that.

PPV/CPV List Building

Another way to generate hundreds of leads per day is through something called Pay Per View or Cost Per View advertising.

I have a friend who does around 1,000 leads a day.

I've only generated 25 leads or so per day with it, but the thing is, is that it's on autopilot.

You can go to a site like leadimpact.com and you can buy cost per view or pay per view advertising.

It's a little different from other types of advertising in that you're paying per view of your page, you're not paying per click on an ad. It's actually more like a pop up, so you're paying for these ads to pop up on people's sites, and it's run through software, so it's different than someone, say going to Google and seeing pay per click ads. You can advertise on any URL on the internet as long as the user has the software installed on their computer. This allows you to bid on different URL's online.
Now you see how this could be popular and profitable because you could bid on your competitor's URL's.

You could bid on so many different URL's it's not even funny.

You could bid on PPC URL's even.

For people who are spending gobs and gobs of money on PPC, you can take those URL's that they're using for their landing pages, plug it into lead impact and then be bidding for ad space for those URL's through the software.

One place to learn more about PPV and CPV is cpvden.com.

It can be a nice little lead flow generator that's different from the other lead flow sources you might be generating leads from right now. What you need to know about also is you can generate tons and tons of traffic for a lot less money, but the traffic won't be as responsive because they didn't click thru to your ad. Because they didn't click through to your ad, it's kind of like an annoying pop up that comes in their face. But, it's all legal and they know they're getting pop ups in exchange for using the software that they're using. It's an agreement they made before downloading the software that they're using on their computer.

If a company, like leadimpact.com, let's say they say, "You can use this software, which has huge value in exchange for being able to run an ad on your computer 5 times per day." Instead of charging for the software each month, they get the software for free, but they have to see ads and this is where your ads can get in front of their face. You can get in front of millions of people for .017 cents each time your ad is shown; that's a fraction of a penny. But, like I said, with other forms of advertising you may get a high opt-in rate on your squeeze page, such as 10% and on some ad sources. 10% is very good. On some ad sources, 10% is horrible. On some ad sources, like solo ads, for example 30% is very good, depending on whether they actually send your solo ad or not because 60% may be considered good on there, as well. But with PPV advertising, we're talking 1-2% could be good, just depending on how much money you're spending, how much money you're making up front and how much money you're making on the backend.

Just because you can get traffic so cheap, it doesn't mean that the traffic is created equal to other advertising sources, because they haven't clicked through any targeted advertising. The traffic responsiveness will be lower, as far as opting into your squeeze page goes.

The point is... all that matters is your ROI, not your opt-in rate... because your opt-in rate is always going to be different, depending on where your traffic is coming from.

Bartering for Leads

Let's discuss bartering for leads.

Bartering for leads is a really great way to generate the highest quality leads you can generate besides having your own product and having an affiliate program. In actuality, it is almost the same or identical to that, except for you are NOT selling your own product.

Here's how it works...

What you want to do is go to a marketer who does product launches, who is bigger than you online. They don't have to be huge; you could just go to someone who does WSO's, for example.

If you go to someone who does WSO's often, you can say this, "I'll do customer service for your launch," or "I'll write the sales page for your launch," or "I'll create bonuses for your launch," or "I'll help create the products for your launch," or "I'll help create buzz using social media for your launch," or "I'll help get JV's on board for your launch" or, "I'll do (something) for your launch in exchange for leads."

You're not asking for money, you're asking for leads.

You're not asking for them export leads to you.
We're talking about just placing some kind of bonus on yours on their download page that customers have to opt-in for, which you get the lead for. For example, this one time I did one of these bartering for leads deals with a top marketer, and for his bonuses on his actual sales page, I advertised my bonuses that they're going to have to opt-in for. On the download page there was a link to my squeeze page, which allowed them to opt-in to download the bonuses. On the page after the squeeze page was the download page for the bonuses. I didn't send them through any kind of sales funnel, but the thing is, you get a list of red-hot buyers when you do this.

Copyright © 2018 Taylor NTerprise LLC

I'm talking about scorching hot buyers.

That first week of having that list you want to promote your highest converting thing, do a webinar or do something that you made money within the past because this is the time to sell them while they're the hottest and they're buyers (you have gained trust by them listening or watching your bonus, depending on what the product is, so they will be responsive). Actually, the way I came up with the bonus for these kinds of launches is I would just use private label rights.

I use private label rights material that was a video course that I didn't even record, but I had rights to give away as a bonus to a paid product.

So that's something to think about.

One of my best tactics was solo ads, one was ad swaps, and at one point click banking. I did click banking on a big scale. Bartering for leads was a huge, huge tactic that I've done before. It works like a charm, and It's not going anywhere. It will always be effective. It's a very simple tactic where you barter your skills with a product launcher who adds your bonus to their download page and the customers have to opt-in for it.

It's not like relying on Google for leads because they can slap that away somehow for you.

And it's not getting less effective like ad swaps are, for example.

Your Own Affiliate Program

Another way to generate red-hot quality leads is by having your own affiliate program.

I'm going to tell you that I've mainly generated leads through using Rapid Action Profits.

I know that a lot of people in recent days have moved on to other scripts, such as Warriorplus.com, WSO Pro or JVZoo.com or DigiResults.com, but I like trusty old Rapid Action Profits.

It may cost $197, whereas I bought it for something like $297.

It's always being updated so it's not out of date with technology or anything, but the reason why I like Rapid Action Profits over any other is two-fold. For one, I only have to pay a fee one time to use it.

I pay my $197 for the script and I use it over and over and over.

A lot of these other sites, you may not have an upfront fee, but they take out fees for every sale you make so you end up paying a lot more than you would pay with that one-time fee to RapidActionProfits.com. There may be, like with WSO Pro, you have to pay a fee every time you want to start a WSO with. I'd rather have a script like Rapid Action Profits so I can use it over and over and over. This is just my personal opinion and preference.

Also, I think there is a lot of wisdom in what I'm about to tell you with Rapid Action Profits vs. the other solutions. The other solutions are like affiliate networks, so when you're recruiting affiliates to actually promote your product, they may end up promoting someone else's product, but with Rapid Action Profits, you have complete control over the situation.

Once you show people your affiliate program, there's only an option to promote you. Therefore, whenever I launch a product on Rapid Action Products, the bottom of the screen I have a link that says, "Affiliates make 100% commissions." They click there and then they sign up for my affiliate program through Rapid Action Profits. They can now get their link and they can then sell the product.

If I use the other programs, and I have a link at the bottom that says, "Sign up here to promote my product," and then they go to some affiliate network, they'll probably end up promoting some other product that they find. They maybe will get lost trying in the sea of products trying to find mine; they give up and not promote any product at all.

The best kind of affiliate program that attracts affiliates is to have an instant PayPal commission affiliate program like the ones I've been talking about.

You can also use something like ClickBank, but you can't give away 100% commissions from ClickBank. With these other programs, you can give away 100% commissions, which is really attractive on the front end to affiliates, and then you can give 50% commission on the one-time offer, for example.

You're making money off sales, but you are attracting affiliates that you don't have to ethically bride much to promote for you.

If you're giving away 100% commissions, in my mind, you're not going to owe any other affiliates back for promoting you because you gave away 100% commissions. Those leads that you get right away are going to be red-hot leads.

Exit Popups

Another way to add about 10% opt-in rate to any website you have is by adding an exit pop up script. You've probably seen these and they're pretty annoying. You can get one at exitsplash.com. When someone tries to leave the page, a pop up will come up that says, "Here's a quick chance to get this freebie," or whatever ad you want there. This can add 10% more opt-in rate to your page or to any website you send traffic to. Actually, depending on how aggressive you want to be, you can have multiple exit pop ups that lead to different squeeze pages.

What I've noticed is in the past, doing a very aggressive launch with a marketer and bartering leads, what I've decided to do with him because he wanted to go balls-to-the-wall, I decided that it would probably be most profitable to do a squeeze page for one offer that pops up once. If they don't take that offer, have a squeeze page that pops up for another offer. If they don't take that offer then another squeeze will pop up for another offer. It will be three squeeze pages popping up in a row for different offers. You will be surprised at how many leads that added onto the product launchers list.

Just think about this, the first squeeze page pops up and they get 10% opt-in rate on that; they've just got 10% of the traffic to sign up on their list. But if they don't take that, and another one pops up and they get 7% on that, well that's an extra 7% tacked on. If they don't take that one though, and they see the third squeeze page up, then maybe 5% tops into that list and all together you've got what, 22% of the people getting on your sales page or site opting into your list. That's almost as good as a decent converting squeeze page. I'll take 22% from a lot of different ad sources depending on the source.

But I will tell you this, that I believe exit pop ups are getting less effective over time because they've been used so much. It's similar to "ad blindness."

What will likely happen is that people will stop using exit pop ups and then wait a little while and then they will start using them again and they will be just as effective as they were before. That's my prediction and that happens to a lot of things where trends and tactics come and go.

Copyright © 2018 Taylor NTerprise LLC

Tactics will be working well, then they stop working as well as they are and everyone stops using them and then someone starts using them again and talking about how profitable it is to use it and then everyone all of a sudden is using it again.

Reverse Opt-in Form

Another way to generate about 10% of your website traffic to your list on a sales page is using a reverse opt-in form. This is where someone clicks on the "Add to Cart" button or an "Order Now" button and then you have a page between your sales page and your order form. That page in between will be a Step 1 of 2 order confirmation form. At the top is will say, "Step 1 of 2 Order Confirmation," then they'll have to put in their email address to continue. This is a Reverse Opt-in Page.

You want to grab the email address here so that everybody who buys your product, you already have then on your list. The people who chicken out on your product, you'll have them on your list and they're also very high-quality subscribers to have on your list that almost buy; for some reason they are.

You might find that the majority of people who actually opt in to that form won't even order, but you'll end up generating a lot more subscribers from your sales page by doing that. You can see how all these leads will add up if you're promoting to a squeeze page or a sales page. You will see how all these leads add up by promoting to a sales page by using all the factors we're talking about here.

If you're getting 22% opt in rates from doing exit pop ups and you're getting 10% from doing reverse opt in forms, then you are generating an extra 33% of people to your subscriber list during a launch.

That's something to think about because when you have all these affiliates hammering your page, a lot of their traffic might not want to buy the product that you have, but there will be people who buy products that you may be able to sell something else to later on as an affiliate or as your own product.

Buying Ad Space Direct from Webmasters

The next tactic I want to talk about is buying ad space directly from webmasters. This can be done as easily as going to different webmasters who have, say forums in your market, and asking how much it would cost to run an ad on the top of their page.

First of all, you're going to them and ask, "How much is your AdSense ad making you on a daily basis?" Chances are you're going to have more money to spend than they're making on this ad from AdSense. They may say, "Well I'm generating 200 people to my site every day, but I'm only making $3.00 in AdSense per day."

If you had an ad that has a 10% click thru rate, then you can generate those people to your page for the same amount of money or more, so tell them that you want to take a test run on their page by advertising their ad in place of their Google ad. You can pay them by PayPal and with a deal like this, "Will you run this ad one day and we'll see how much money I make," and you'll give them $5 instead of the $3.00 he makes from AdSense, for example.

Then, you see what happens when you run your ad on their site for that day and see how many opt ins you get, how much in sales in commissions you make from your sales funnel, and this will determine whether it's profitable or not. If it's profitable then you can say, "Well I would like to rent that ad space from you on a monthly basis, for the rest of this month for x amount of dollars," or whatever is equivalent to $5.00 a day, or whatever you're testing. If you go to some real busy forum, for example, and you do the same thing – and if we're talking about bigger numbers here, maybe you will do a $50 test run for one day. You measure the results and see what happens and if it works out well, then what you need to do is just tell them that you want to run an ad that month for x amount of dollars. And that's traffic you don't have to touch. That's just autopilot traffic hitting your page. You can run it on a weekly basis or anything that you can afford, but the point is these webmasters want to make more money on their sites because they're probably not making as much as you can give them using the advertising that they're running.

Copyright © 2018 Taylor NTerprise LLC

They're making piss poor profits from AdSense, for example.

Actually, in the internet marketing space, WarriorForum.com has an option to run an ad at the top of the forum for $100 a day, and they run something like eight different spaces on there a day and yours would rotate with eight different advertisers. That's a good way to test something in the internet marketing niche.

If you want to test an ad out and see how internet marketers would respond before you go and promote something on internet marketing, then use the tactic of contacting vendors and webmasters directly and you could run a $100 ad and see what happens. Chances are you could get at least $100 clicks of traffic, or you may get 50 to 100 opt-ins. You may get one sale at $100 that makes you break even.

You never know.

You never know until you try, but what I like about this media buying approach is that it's very easy traffic that you don't have to work toward, you just have to monitor your metrics.

Nested Squeeze Page on Blog

Here's a tactic for generating a lot of leads from a blog. I actually built my first list of 1,000 subscribers this way in the guitar niche before I even got into the internet marketing niche.

It's so easy.

You take a blog and maybe your blog is generating 100, 200, 300 visitors per day because you're cranking content out on a daily basis. Even if you don't try to target certain keywords on your site, it's pretty easy to start generating 200 to 300 visitors per day just by cranking out content and ranking it for long tail search terms without even trying to, and actually only doing it. You take your squeeze page in your niche, and you nest it at the top and center of that blog.

Before they actually see the blog site at the top of the page, they should see your squeeze page as it is. You can nest it up there using an image and an opt in box, if you want. That's if you don't want the test of the squeeze page to interfere with any other on page SEO that's happening. You'll be surprised at the opt-in rate you can get from that.

Let's say your site isn't really an interactive site as much as you want it to be; it's really difficult to get a site with a lot of interactivity. Maybe your site just has a lot of traffic coming to it and doesn't really have people interacting, so it doesn't really matter if you put your squeeze page up there or not.

One of the best ways to generate leads form a blog is to nest a squeeze page front and center. Another way is by using Robert Plank's WordPress Plug-Ins. One is called Action Opt-In. This is where you can put an opt-in bar on your side bar that you go opt-in to. Once they opt-in to it, the form will disappear and say, "Thanks for subscribing," and keep the people on the blog they're on. One is Action Pop-Up, which is a fade in window that fades into your site and asks for the opt-in there in exchange for a freebie or whatever you're offering. The other is Action Comments, which is where if someone comments on your blog, they check a check box and it automatically subscribes them to your list. You can get all three, I believe, in one purchase from Robert Plank if you go to Actionoptin.com or search on Google for Action Opt-In and you'll probably find it. He's always updating that.

Tell-A-Friend Script

Another way to generate leads virally is by using a Tell-A-Friend script.

I think you have to be careful not to let others abuse your Tell-A-Friend script because they can go spamming the Internet with it, but I think the best practice for using a Tell-A-Friend script is to have one on your download page for your freebie that you just giveaway. It will say, "I'll give you this extra bonus if you tell 5 friends about this," or "10 friends about this." There will be a little form that they fill out and they'll type in five different email addresses, for example, of their friends and when they hit submit it will send out a message to all their friends from them, which tells them to go and check out your squeeze page basically. It's really good traffic because they're endorsing you, in a way. They are friends of friends recommending you to other friends to your site, which is better than running an ad on some site where no one knows you, no authority is being transferred to you, or not trust is being transferred to you. You may be able to get really good leads by doing so. Mike Filsaime has a Tell-A-Friend script and there are other ones out there on the market that you can search for in Google by searching for Tell-A-Friend script. I have a feeling those will also be on the rise in the future. Those are one of those tactics that were used a lot years ago and you don't see them as much anymore, but I think that they will emerge again, especially when people start using them in a way that makes the person who's sending out the Tell-A-Friend script use their own email server to mail out the Tell-A-Friend invitation, that way they can avoid spam troubles altogether.

The worse way to use a Tell-A-Friend script is if you're telling people to send out one of their affiliate links and they're an affiliate for you because then they may spam your site a lot because they're trying to make money. They may get excited, they might be spammers, or they might just get a little too excited and start sending it out to everybody and everyone they can find, thinking they're going to make a million dollars overnight.

Integrated Cross-Promotions

I want to talk about generating leads is using integrated cross-promotions. I think Mark Joyner coined the term integrated marketing. Well integrated cross-promotions are different kinds of cross promos that you have with your joint venture partners other than ad swaps, click banking, or anything like JV giveaways. These are different because these are integrated into your marketing on autopilot, so you to think about the different parts of your marketing systems that you can integrate some kind of joint venture link to.

For example, on your download page, you might have a banner that leads to one of your JV partner's squeeze pages and they have the same for you on their download page. That would be an example of an integrated cross- promotion. Instead of monetizing that part of your download page with an offer, what you'll do is do an integrated cross-promotion with one of your joint venture partners.

Another way is to cross promote your joint venture partner in your follow up series. In your email follow up series, maybe your fifth email in the follow up series will promote their squeeze page and their fifth email in their follow up series will promote your squeeze page.

Another way is through P.S.'s of your emails that you send out. When you're sending out an email to your list, you can make a deal with one of your joint venture partners to always promote their squeeze page in their P.S. and they have to do the same for you. That's one way to do it.

Think about the power of integrated cross-promotion. You're generating subscribers on autopilot by doing this. You can add tons per day to your list or more, all on autopilot, by doing this a set of joint venture partners or with just one, but just think about this; let's say you have 10 joint venture partners and you're going to do integrated joint venture cross-promotions with your follow up series of emails. If 10 of you, in all 10 of your first follow up series emails, promote each other, visitors would be flying all over the place and going onto your list.

Viral PDF Reports

The next tactic I want to talk about is using viral PDF reports. Let's say you write a little report that can be 2 to 5 pages long, as long as it's rock solid content; it's going to be for a free report anyway, and you create a PDF report out of it. Inside the PDF report, you want to say that this is free to distribute. Also, inside of your PDF report, you want to have a link at the end that leads to your squeeze page or an entire ad that leads to your squeeze page.

What I've found in the past is that other people started using my reports to build their lists with. They would actually give my l reports away to their squeeze pages and I would generate those subscribers under my list, the ones who actually read the report and then clicked thru at the end. The ones who read the reports and clicked through to the end and discovered you that way, end up being some of the highest quality leads you'll get because they've just read one of your reports, and they clicked through at the end to get your freebie, and you've got them on your list. If you're not sure how to do this, you can go to OpenOffice online.

- You can just type into Google, "OpenOffice" and download OpenOffice Writer.

- You're going to open up OpenOffice Writer and write your report. It's kind of like Microsoft Word.

- Then you're going to click "File" and export as a PDF.

Once you do that, you have a PDF that you can give away, and you have clickable links inside the PDF and that will become your viral report. It's a little different than re-brandable reports. If you have your own affiliate program, you can give affiliates a way to give cool content to their list and to promote you at the same time by offering a viral brandable rewritable report. This is a little bit different, a little more simplistic, and if you give enough of these reports away that are viral reports, you may see them circulating all over the place and generating leads from all over the internet.

Affiliate List Cross-Promotions

The last thing I want to tell you about list building is using affiliate list cross-promotions.

This is very simple.

Let's say you have your own offer on Rapid Action Profits and you've built an affiliate list, which is just a list of affiliates who promote your profits. What you do is you go to other product owners who have affiliate lists and you say, "I will tell my affiliate list about your affiliate program if you do the same for yours." You might pick up some really good affiliates like that. They might pick up a few and once you pick up affiliates, that means more traffic heading into your paid offer, which means more people on your list of high quality.

This is one of those tactics that kind of make you want to slap yourself in the head.

End of Lesson 1

Copyright © 2018 Taylor NTerprise LLC

Lesson 2

Niche Marketing
Resource Guide
By Kevin Taylor

Copyright © 2018 Taylor NTerprise LLC

Part 1: Getting Niche Ideas

This report is split into two sections. The first section is all about getting niche ideas. Once you have a nice list of niche ideas, section two will help you analyze the list of niches and "prune" it down to only the most profitable niches.

This short guide may aid you in your internet marketing journeys. You may want to use it as a resource guide whenever you're looking to expand your business, so keep it on your desktop or somewhere it'll be easy to find. It's taken years and lots of experience to learn these methods and resources that are compiled all into this one report.

Niche ideas are all around you, offline and online.

I'm about to share with you 21 resources and ways to get good ideas for niches. Get out a pad and a pen and make a list of potential niches because you're about to discover literally thousands of them. I want you to write down the ones you resonate with.

Sure, there are profitable niches everywhere, but the niche you choose should be something you're at least interested in or already know about. You don't need to be an absolute expert in a niche to break into it. However, it helps to have interest in it since you'll be doing business in that niche every day. If a niche bores you to death, then not only will it be hard to get motivated to do any work, but your lack of passion will show to potential customers and website visitors.

Another thing to consider is to choose only a niche that you feel comfortable with. For example, Gambling niches are very profitable, but you may or may not feel comfortable with it. The same goes for any other niche you may not be comfortable with such as Pay Day Loans. It's lucrative, but if you can't sleep well at night promoting pay day loan offers, then don't touch that niche even with a 50-foot pole.

Niche Discovery Resource #1:
Magazines.com

For hobby niche ideas, check out Magazines.com and browse the various categories.

If there's enough interest in a subject that there's a popular magazine based around it, then you may have a profitable niche on your hands!

If you happen to have a subscription to any of the magazines at magazines.com, then you can find great niche ideas by checking out the paid ads inside the magazines.

Niche Discovery Resource #2:
Offer Vault

You can search CPA offers that will give you plenty of niche ideas at Offer Vault.

One of the best parts about Offer Vault is that you don't even have to search for anything to get profitable niche ideas.

Right when you land on the site, you'll see the offers that are paying the highest per lead.

Niche Discovery Resource #3:
Amazon Best Sellers

You can get good physical product niche ideas by checking out the Amazon Best Sellers list. You can browse the best selling products in any category.

You may want to take a look at for niche ideas is the Table of Contents of best selling books by using the "Look Inside" feature on Amazon.com. There are sub-niches galore to be discovered inside the tables of contents of these books.

Copyright © 2018 Taylor NTerprise LLC

Niche Discovery Resource #4:
National Enquirer Ads

The National Enquirer has the most expensive ad space of any print publication, so pay attention to the ads you see inside each issue you read.

If advertisers are paying that kind of money to run their ads, then the offers they're running must be hot. Take a look at what they're advertising in these mega expensive advertisements because where there are hot offers, there are hot niche ideas.

Niche Discovery Resource #5:
eBay Pulse

You can get some great niche ideas by checking out eBay Pulse, which will tell you the most popular searches and trends on eBay.

You can also browse categories and stores on eBay to spark niche ideas. The categories section is one of the most in-depth I've seen, so give it a look and see what niches are out there.

Niche Discovery Resource #6:
Dummies.com

I'm sure you've seen the "For Dummies" books over the years. If a subject has profit potential, then they make a book about it. What most internet marketers don't know is that Dummies.com is an excellent place to get niche ideas by browsing the various "For Dummies" books.

Niche Discovery Resource #7:
BoardReader

One great way to find out what people are talking about on forums is by using a forum search engine like BoardReader. Type in a topic like "Weight Loss" and find out what people are talking about in various forum threads. Pay attention to the problems they're talking about and get niches ideas. People pay for solutions to problems.

Niche Discovery Resource #8:
Flippa

Flippa is a massive marketplace for buying and selling websites.

As you look through the marketplace, pay attention to the expensive sites and ones that are making a profit because if those sites are making a profit, then why can't you have a site in the same niche that makes a profit as well?

You can actually reverse engineer these websites in a way, to find out how their links were built, what type of content they have, and who their audience is by using a tool like Quantcast.

Niche Discovery Resource #9:
Clickbank Marketplace

If you're a digital products marketer then you no doubt already know about ClickBank and the ClickBank Marketplace. Besides internet marketing related products, the CB Marketplace is a great place to find niches based on Gravity. Each product in the marketplace has a Gravity Score (Grav), which is a measurement of how many affiliates have had success promoting a product, so you can find some profitable niches by looking at the products with the highest Gravity.

Niche Discovery Resource #10:
JVZoo

JVZoo is a newer affiliate network, but growing by leaps and bounds. I predict it will become one of the major affiliate networks for digital goods across all niches, so you should join and take a look at the products in the marketplace. The best part about JVZoo is you can see the $ Per Click (the Earnings Per Click) of each product, so the higher the EPC, the higher converting it is. Products with the highest EPCs may give you good ideas for niches that have high converting products.

Niche Discovery Resource #11:
Pay Dot Com

You can find niche ideas by also browsing the Pay Dot Com marketplace. Pay Dot Com is another digital products affiliate network like ClickBank and JVZoo, bigger than JVZoo yet smaller than ClickBank.

The best niche ideas you can get from Pay Dot Com will come from the Top Sellers section.

Niche Discovery Resource #12:
Recurring TV Infomercials

You may or may not be a fan of infomercials, but nonetheless, they are great for conjuring up niche ideas! When you see an infomercial running multiple times, then chances are that infomercial is profitable. Try to figure out who the ideal customer is for that product.

You can actually promote many of these products you see in infomercials in CPA networks like Wolf Storm Media.

Niche Discovery Resource #13:
Google Trends

You'll get a good idea of what topics are hot at any given moment by using Google Trends. It's also a good idea to type in subjects such as "weight loss" into Google Trends, because you'll find related news articles.

You can get some great niche ideas from those news articles. Just beware that trends come and go, obviously, so you may not want to base an entire business on trends.

Niche Discovery Resource #14:
Yahoo! Answers

When you're looking to find out what kind of problems people are having and what solutions they're looking for, Yahoo! Answers can be an almost magical tool. If you have no idea what you're looking for, then you can browse categories to find potential niche ideas. If you have a question in mind, then type it into the search box to see what related questions people are asking, and try to find the most pressing problems.

Niche Discovery Resource #15:
Shopping.com Popular Pages

Shopping.com is where consumers go to compare products. You'll get niche ideas by exploring their list of Most Popular Products and Popular Pages.

Here's one I found that I never would've thought of on my own: Wedding Corsages.

Niche Discovery Resource #16:
Yahoo! Shopping

Yahoo! Shopping can give you great ideas for profitable niches with their Shopping Insider articles. Looking at the front page right now I'm getting ideas like Prom Styles and Valentine's Day Gifts.

Browse articles by category and you'll end up with a good list of possible niches.

Niche Discovery Resource #17:
Ezinearticles.com

Although Ezinearticles.com got drilled by Google's Panda update, it is still a massive resource for niche ideas for you to take a look at. You'll get niche ideas by browsing different categories and seeing what these authors are writing about.

If a particular author has many posts, pay attention to what subjects he or she is writing about because nobody writes that many articles for no reason. There may be profit potential.

Copyright © 2018 Taylor NTerprise LLC

Niche Discovery Resource #18:
Google Keyword Tool

The Google Keyword tool can be used to find sub-niches galore. (Do a Google search for "Google Keyword Tool").

When you have a keyword like "weight loss," type it into the Google Keyword tool, then select "only show ideas closely related to my search terms."

You'll start to see long-tail keywords related to the keyword that will begin to dig deeper and find sub-niches.

Niche Discovery Resource #19:
AdSense Sandbox

AdSense Sandbox is a fun site that will show you AdSense ads that are running on sites related to the subject you submit.

When you see the ads that are running and what products and services are being promoted, you should start getting good niche ideas.

Pay close attention to the similarities of products because you may be onto something if you see the same type of product over and over.

Niche Discovery Resource #20:
Bottom Line Publications

If you're looking for niche ideas related to Health in particular, then Bottom Line Publications is an excellent resource. When you go to the site, browse the subjects of their books and newsletters because they are bigtime direct marketers.

If these niches are responsive to their direct marketing tactics, then they may be responsive to yours as well.

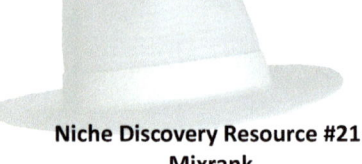

Niche Discovery Resource #21:
Mixrank

Mixrank will show you PPC ads that are running in various niches when you submit an advertiser, keyword, or publisher into the field. The best part is Mixrank will tell you how long an ad has been running.

The longer an ad has been running, generally the more profitable that offer is, so you can see how you can get some niche ideas that are more likely to be profitable. There's a free and a paid version, but the paid version is unnecessary with what we're trying to accomplish here.

Part 2:
Pruning Your List of Niches

By now, you should have a monster list of potentially profitable niches if you went through each resource. No worries if your list is small from only using a couple of the resources.

Now we're going to take your list and "prune it." We'll prune it down to the niches of your liking by analyzing them. We're not going to analyze them by using exact data or an exact science.

No niche is perfect, but there are many things to consider when deciding to do internet marketing in a niche. The most important part of this process is finding out the things that appeal most to YOU when it comes to each niche. Use the following 21 Questions when determining whether a niche is for you or not. Some of the questions are about the profit potential of a niche. Other questions are about how easy it's going to be for you to reach your target audience on a daily basis.

Then there are questions about how fast you can grow and become a force in any given niche market. If a niche doesn't sit with you after asking these 21 questions then delete it from your list. By the end you will have a handful of niches left to choose from.

Keep in mind that there are more questions than just these 21 questions you can consider when selecting a niche. These happen to be the questions that are important to me based on my experience with internet marketing.

Besides having a general interest in a niche and being comfortable with it ethically, I want a niche to have profit potential, potential to generate easy traffic, and potential for fast growth.

Question #1:
Are there multiple products in the niche?

The first question you want to ask yourself is, are there a lot of good products? You want to know this because you may quickly run out of good products to offer to your website visitors or e-mail list subscribers. If you're running AdSense or selling ad space on your website or selling ad space in your e-mail newsletter, then that's one thing. But if you're going to be depending on making commissions, then it's vital to have multiple offers you can promote.

Question #2:
How big is the problem your prospect is having?

If it's not a hobby niche, how big is the problem the prospects are having?

Is the problem they're having big enough that they'd be willing to part with their hard-earned money to get a solution?

Maybe someone would be willing to pay for pain relief, but they wouldn't be willing to pay to solve a lesser problem.

Question #3:
Are there potential JV partners in the niche for explosive growth?

Here's something not many marketers consider when selecting a niche. Are there potential Joint Venture partners already in the niche? Are all of them so big that they would never consider doing a JV deal with you? Or, are they so small that it wouldn't matter if they did a JV deal with you?

There's no faster way to grow a business than by using Joint Venture deals, so it's something to consider.

Question #4:
Does it make sense to build a list in the niche or not?

Are other internet marketers in the niche building an e-mail subscriber list?

Would it make sense to build a list in the niche?

You may or may not want to get into a niche where it's a must to build a list in order to make nice profits. Take a look around at the competitors and see if they have opt-in forms on their websites or not. Join their lists and see what it would be like to market in that niche.

Question #5:
How expensive is available ad inventory in the niche?

One major thing you have to consider before getting into a new niche is how easy it will be to reach your target audience.

If you're looking to pay for traffic, then you'll want to see how expensive the ad inventory is for that market. For example, you'll find the costs vary when bidding on keywords and URLs using CPV networks like LeadImpact and also when bidding on PPC keywords with Google AdWords.

Question #6:
Will it be easy to generate free traffic in this niche?

If you're looking at going the free traffic route, then take a look around at how easy (or hard) it would be to reach your target prospects in a particular niche using free methods. You can use the Google Keyword Tool to discover generally how competitive keywords are in a niche.

Try to do some digging around and find out if your competitors are successfully using other free sources like YouTube, Twitter, and Facebook.

If they can do it, then why not you?

Question #7:
Are there high-end products or services at $1,000 or more in the niche?

Are there products or services being sold at $1,000, $5,000, or even $10,000 in a niche?

Not many niches have customers who actively spend $1,000 or more on a single product or service. If you can find many offers in your niche in those price ranges, then that's a good sign that you can make easy money in your niche.

In a niche where high-end products are being sold often, you'll find it's easier to make 1 sale at $1,000 than 100 sales at $10.

Question #8:
Are there continuity programs like membership sites in the niche?

It's easier to make dependable income when there are continuity programs in a niche. I'm talking about membership sites, subscriptions, etc. They are especially lucrative when there are services that customers need and will keep paying for month after month. This is where webhosting and auto-responder services come into play.

Question #9:
How fast do vendors pay out in the niche and do they pay out at all?

When vendors don't pay out fast or if they don't pay at all, then that can cripple your business in itself. That's why I recommend staying away from any affiliate programs that aren't on networks like ClickBank, for the most part. There are exceptions to the rule.

Many product vendors wait up to 90 days to pay out commissions, and many don't pay out at all because either they're dirty or they're not responsible enough with their money.

If the only available affiliate programs in your niche aren't on affiliate networks then my advice is to avoid them like the plague.

Question #10:

Copyright © 2018 Taylor NTerprise LLC

Are exact match domains available in the niche?

While this isn't a must, it can give you an edge when it comes to free traffic from Google.

An exact match domain is a domain name (.com preferably) that matches a keyword you want to rank for in Google.

One easy way to find whether there are exact match domains available in your niche is to take your keyword list and copy and paste it into GoDaddy Bulk Domain Register.

You can use that feature on GoDaddy to find out whether there are exact match domains available without actually buying the domains through GoDaddy.

Question #11:
Could you create a product in this niche?

Having your own product gives you maximum leverage in a niche.

You can create cross promotion deals with JV partners and you can sit back and let your affiliate army crush your offer with traffic all day long.

If it's a physical product you must create in a niche, then that may be something you can't do.

As for digital products, if you don't have the expertise in a niche, then there may be Private Label Rights material available on the web that you can use to aid you in creating a respectable product.

Question #12:
Will it be easy to build your authority in the niche?

Having your own product is honestly the ultimate way to build authority in a niche.

Another way is by having JV partners who customers associate you with, so you're borrowing your JV partner's credibility in a way.

A popular blog can also give you authority in a niche. Are there already authority blogs in the niche you're looking at? If so, then you may also be able to have one yourself.

Question #13:
Do you already have knowledge of this niche?

It's much easier to enter a niche when you already have knowledge or expertise in it. You don't have to be an expert, but being an intermediate is enough to share what you know information-wise. If you have a burning desire to learn more about a niche, then that can help in entering a niche as well. In that role, you're more of a reporter than an authority figure.

Question #14:
Are people spending money in this niche?

Many hobbies are popular and solutions for problems are searched for all over the net, but that doesn't mean they spend money on it. In this case, you'll need to verify whether there are buyers in the niche or not by checking out bestseller lists using the resources in Part 1.

It's easy to make the mistake of choosing a popular yet unprofitable niche, so make sure you "do your homework" on this.

Question #15:
Is coaching being sold in the niche?

Everyone knows there's good money to be made in coaching, whether internet marketing coaching, life coaching, etc.

Coaching packages are sold for thousands of dollars, so if you're a good lead generator then you can either sell your own coaching packages or generate leads for coaches who do sell packages. They can afford to spend more on leads you generate for them because they're charging high prices.

Copyright © 2018 Taylor NTerprise LLC

Question #16:
Are there pay per lead offers in this niche?

Promoting Pay Per Lead Offers can be much more profitable than Pay Per Sale Offers, which you may be accustomed to. It's easier to get someone to fill out a form than buy something.

If there are Pay Per Lead Offers in the niche, then you may have an easier time converting your traffic into money.

Question #17:
Will it be easy to stand out from the crowd in this niche?

Some niches have a crazy amount of competition, but that doesn't mean you should be scared to enter them.

Is there a way you can stand out from the crowd in a competitive niche?

Think about it, because standing out can help you stomp your competition into the ground. This has a lot to do with positioning. Maybe you have expertise in a sub-niche that you can share that will put you head and shoulders above your competition.

Question #18:
Are there webinars or teleseminars in the niche?

Webinars and teleseminars generate sales like crazy, but not every niche is responsive to them.

In any niche you need a vehicle to make money, so if there are webinars and teleseminars in a niche, then chances are you can do the same thing or promote them as an affiliate. While the average conversion rate of a sales letter online is roughly 1%, webinars and teleseminars convert generally around 10% or more.

Question #19:
Are there call centers in this niche?

What converts even higher than webinars and teleseminars, is one-on-one phone selling, so keep an eye out for it in the niche you're assessing. Just beware that many call centers are dirty.

However, just using the phone to sell will increase your conversion rates to as much as 50% depending on how the lead was generated.

If there are call centers in a niche, then you can also use the power of the telephone to close more sales.

Question #20:
Is this niche related to Health, Wealth, or Relationships?

If the niche you're looking at is related to Health, Wealth, or Relationships, then you may have a mass market on your hands.

Health, Wealth, and Relationships-related products and services are known to be cash cows.

The traffic potential is generally higher when related to Health, Wealth, and Relationships.

Question #21:
Are there many searches in Google in this niche?

Take a look at the Google Keyword Tool (type "Google Keyword Tool" into Google to find it). If you see low traffic levels for keywords in your niche, then it doesn't make much sense to choose this niche.

Sure, the competition is likely low. However, there's usually a reason for that, there are a lack of customers.

END OF LESSON 2

Copyright © 2018 Taylor NTerprise LLC

Lesson 3
Paid Traffic
Bargain Hunter
By Kevin Taylor

Copyright © 2018 Taylor NTerprise LLC

Introduction

There are some nice new advertising sources in this report for you to discover and some of them are huge. Others are smaller yet legit. I'm talking about Solo Ads, PPC, PPV, as well as some untraditional types of advertising like paying for blog posts.

I hope you'll find many new ad networks and places to buy ads from that you didn't previously know about. It's important to note that you're not going to need all of these sources. You could spend millions of dollars with just one or a handful of these select sources.

Think of this report as like a mini guide to the available ad inventory out there that you may have not known about. Crack it open whenever you're looking to buy some traffic.

Before we get started with these ad sources, I also wanted to tell you that you can get a world-class education in buying traffic for free. One way is to join a CPA network such as Wolf Storm Media and take their free trainings. Another way is to learn all you can from the actual ad network sites that you'll discover in this report. It's also vital to get some ads running and track everything using a program such as Prosper 202.

You honestly don't need a $2,000 course to learn about internet advertising because the best way to learn is to get out there and do it. While you can learn the basics from someone else, the real learning comes from your experience.

When you're tweaking ads, when you're tweaking your bids, when you're crunching your numbers and looking at your metrics and adjusting... That's when you're REALLY learning!

Take everything you learn from others like a grain of salt. Take these advertising sources, go out there, and generate all the traffic your little heart desires.

Copyright © 2018 Taylor NTerprise LLC

JV Rocket and "Tier 1 Solo Ads"

With JV Rocket, you can buy a solo ad that will go out to a double opt-in list of 226,000 subscribers for the price of $2,500. Your ad goes out to customers who have purchased ClickBank products in the Make Money niche such as Get Google Ads Free, Health Biz in a Box, Forced Money, and Top Secret Magic Code.

You'll also reach affiliates for ClickBank products such as Get Google Ads Free, Health Biz in a Box, Forced Money, Top Secret Magic Code, Cash Making Power Sites, Top Secret Fat Loss Secret, and Top Secret Car Secret.

Many of the top Internet Marketing and Make Money niche gurus are using JV Rocket to build their lists and also to directly mail to their hot offers. $2,500 is a nice chunk of money to risk, so before testing a JV Rocket you'll want to make sure you have tested sales material.

You'll also want to be sure that your offer would be a good match for the type of customers who would buy the type of products I just mentioned above. This doesn't mean that your offers must be similar, but it does mean that the same demographic would order your product.

The downside of this solo ad source is that there are no guaranteed amount of visitors you'll get. The upside is that if you have an offer that's on fire and would work well with these types of customers then JV Rocket can be a goldmine.

Just remember, as with all of these ad sources in this report, you're responsible for your business and the risks you take with buying advertising.

Profiting from paid advertising is simple, but not easy.

It would be easier to blow through $10,000 on JV Rockets. The inventory is there waiting for you to order anytime you want. However, it would be wise to test your sales funnel out buying solo ads on a small scale at $30, $100, or $300 a pop from "Tier 2 Solo Ad" vendors such as the ones on Safe-Swaps.com, SoloAdDirectory.com, or Directory of Ezines.

Copyright © 2018 Taylor NTerprise LLC

After you have a tested and proven funnel that works well with the solo ads you've purchased on a small scale, then you may want to consider going big time and ordering what I call "Tier 1 Solo Ads" such as JV Rocket.

JV Rocket isn't the only Tier 1 Solo Advertising available. Here are some more in various niches: Arcamax (General Consumer List), Newsmax, Self Growth, and Nextmark.

LeadImpact and Top CPV Networks

Technically TrafficVance is a better quality CPV network than LeadImpact in my opinion, but the barrier to entry with TrafficVance is $1,000. With LeadImpact, on the other hand, you only need $100 to get started using their massive network.

I find it much easier to generate mass targeted traffic with LeadImpact than the other major CPV networks with a low barrier to entry such as Direct CPV and Media Traffic.

LeadImpact allows you to buy traffic on a Per View basis. You're essentially buying something similar to popups. Paying "Per View" means a small window will open on their screen and it will lead to your webpage. Your webpage must fit inside that window. (To test whether your webpage will fit inside the window, use something like this free tool.)

You can bid on keywords or URLs using LeadImpact. When bidding on a keyword, website content will match your keyword and trigger your pop up. When bidding on a URL, visiting that URL will trigger your popup. Depending on your Geo Targeting and the Category/Sub-Category of your offer, the lowest bid you can start with will be as low as .015 to .017.

The downside of LeadImpact is that I don't personally like how they have the minimum bidding set up. For some Sub-Categories you might have a minimum bid of .015 and for others it may be .025. One cent may not seem like a big difference but when you multiply that 1,000+ times per day, it starts to add up. Small squeeze pages seem to do very well with LeadImpact. They can be your own squeeze pages or a Pay-Per-Lead (PPL) offer in a CPA network.

I find there's not as much inventory in the Make Money and Internet Marketing niches, but there's a ton in large markets that are multiple times bigger. For example, you can generate a serious amount of traffic on a daily basis to Pay-Per-Lead online gaming offers. Same goes for Weight Loss, Health, and Financial niches.

To find PPL offers to promote, try a CPA offers search engine such as Offer Vault.

Copyright © 2018 Taylor NTerprise LLC

Plenty of Fish Ads

With Plenty of Fish ads, you can reach 20,000,000 users on a CPM basis.

In case you're not familiar with "CPM," it simply means "Cost per 1,000 impressions of your ad." You'll also be bidding for ad inventory on a CPM basis. The minimum buy is just $25, so you can cheaply give POF Ads a nice test run for as low as $25. It takes 24 hours or less for your ads to be approved. Image ad sizes include 110x80px, 300x250px, 160x600px and 120x600.

Besides the insanely low point of entry at $25 minimum, there's something else about POF Ads that makes your traffic highly targeted. In-depth demographics targeting is available. You can target prospects based on: Country, State/Province, Zip Code, Age, Gender, Education, Profession, Has Children, Games and Puzzles, Body Type, Drinking Habits, Looking to Marry Soon, Ethnicity, Height, Income, Login Count, Marital Status, Religion, Search Type, Smoking Habits, Session Depth, Hair Color, and Has Car (or not). Your ads are so ultra-targeted that they're not even shown to POF visitors who aren't logged in. Your ad is displayed above the fold as well.

With POF Ads you can really go to town with specific dating offers. For instance, imagine targeting Christians who are looking to date. You can put a Christian Singles offer in front of them.

Do you see how powerful POF Ads can be?

Because you have access to so many demographics, your ads don't even have to be about dating. They can be about something totally unrelated, but targeted to the demographic you choose.

There are many CPA offers out there related to dating if that's what you want to explore. This is a perfect time for you to start your Dating or Relationships niche empire by generating leads from Plenty Of Fish to your own subscriber list.

ClickBank products such as The Magic of Making Up may also do well with POF Ads.

Copyright © 2018 Taylor NTerprise LLC

7Search, Ad Hitz, and LinkedIn Ads

7Search is one of my favorite of the "Tier 2 PPC" networks, search engines, and the like. Google, Yahoo, MSN, and Facebook are considered "Tier 1 PPC" in my book. Everything else is Tier 2 PPC the way I see it.

The great thing about 7Search is you don't have to worry about Quality Score or other headaches. You set up a landing page, you bid on keywords, and you tweak your campaigns until they're profitable.

If you're looking to generate Biz Opp leads, then you may want to check out Ad Hitz. With Ad Hitz, you can do Site Specific Targeting (recommended) on some biz opp sites that get serious traffic, such as MyBrowserCash.com that gets 23,1411 unique visitors per day and ClickSense.com that gets 281,360 unique visitors per day.

Now, if you're looking for serious Internet Marketing niche leads, then Ad Hitz may or may not be for you. The leads you generate will be the type that hang out on pay to click sites and probably paid survey sites. This doesn't necessarily mean that these prospects are "low quality" or not serious about business, but it does mean that they're clueless about what you and I know about. Therefore, I think it's important to not take advantage of these clueless prospects. Instead, you should show them the light.

For serious Internet Marketing leads who are already more advanced, you'll want to buy an ad at the top of WarriorForum.com or run Warrior Special Offers. There are over 450,000 members on Warrior Forum and growing.

Another option for generating serious Business leads in general is by using LinkedIn Ads. You won't necessarily generate all internet marketing leads there, but there are 130,000,000 business-minded members on LinkedIn to advertise to. 40,000,000 are US based.

With LinkedIn Ads you don't have to pay on a PPC basis because they also offer inventory on a CPM basis (cost per 1,000 impressions). It's your choice.

Copyright © 2018 Taylor NTerprise LLC

PayPerPost, Blog Ads, and ReviewMe

You may want to consider blog advertising. This is where your website or your product is promoted on real blogs.

PayPerPost is one of them and they connect you with real bloggers out there who are willing to do a write up about your product or site for a fee. Besides generating the direct traffic from your links, you'll also be building links, except you won't be building links on fly-by-night blog networks that get de-indexed from the search engines in the blink of an eye. You have complete control over how much you'll spend on a post when you create your listing called an "Opportunity." You also get to select the categories and the Geo Targeting.

Blog Ads is another option for advertising on blogs, but it's not contextual like PayPerPost. Here you're buying actual ad space on a time basis. You're not buying on a PPC or CPM basis like some of the other sources we've talked about. You're buying ads based on the amount of time they'll run on the blog. It's just like buying ad space direct from a webmaster at a fixed rate, only you're doing it through the Blog Ads network. The pricing is set up similar to Text-Link-Ads. Price doesn't go up or down based on the amount of impressions or click throughs on your ad.

ReviewMe is another option with blog advertising and it can work well to create buzz for your new product or service. You can browse the different blogs at ReviewMe.com and purchase a review of your product or service. You'll also get the link back to your site, but just keep in mind that these bloggers will do an honest review for you and that review will be permanent. You can also create a listing for what you're looking for if you're looking to be found by bloggers who are looking to review products or services similar to your own.

AbestWeb, CB, JV Zoo, W+, PDC, DigiResults

If you're advertising to get affiliates, then you'll want to run some ads on AbestWeb, the world's largest affiliate marketing forum. Super affiliates galore hang out on this forum and have their eyes open for hot offers to promote all the time. They can generate traffic all day long, but they don't always have offers that convert, so if your offer is appealing enough to them, then just one super affiliate you get from running an ad can be worth much more than what you paid for the ad.

To read about the different advertising options at AbestWeb, check out this page. They have all kinds of inventory from banner ads to e-mail blasts to their members.

Getting your digital product listed in the ClickBank Marketplace is also a great way to pick up affiliates who can drive traffic to your site all day and night on a commission basis. With ClickBank, you're technically buying traffic, but it's no risk because you're only paying when someone makes a sale. Other options have emerged as well including JV Zoo, WSO Pro, PayDotCom, and DigiResults.

Honestly, I'm a fan of all those programs just listed. Instead of being paid by ClickBank, you're paid directly upon each sale with PayPal. However, the marketplaces aren't even close to as old or as big as ClickBank.

There are a lot more affiliates waiting in the ClickBank marketplace to see your offer to promote than the others, but you don't get instant PayPal payments.

You can also pick up some affiliates by listing your product in the Warrior Forum Affiliate Programs Database for a small fee.

There are more ways to get super affiliates to promote for you. One is by busting your butt putting together a massive product launch and getting listed on sites like JV Notify Pro and Warrior JV. Another way is to simply get the attention of super affiliates by running your offer on networks.

If you throw $10,000 at advertising your offer, then chances are super affiliates are going to see it, and they are always looking for one thing: offers that convert.

Stumbleupon Ads, PR Web, and Direct CPV

If you know how StumbleUpon works, it's where users click the "Stumble" button and they are sent from webpage to webpage checking out pages that have been "Stumbled" by other users and are related to their favorite topics. With StumbleUpon Paid Discovery, your webpage becomes part of that Stumbling process. Users land on your landing page while Stumbling through websites and you pay per view. My opinion is it's a bit pricey at this point, but I also think it's a great way for companies to spread brand awareness and it's also potentially good for viral marketing.

Using PR Web is another way to launch a viral marketing or brand awareness campaign. To tell you the truth, it's also possible to generate a lot of direct traffic as well, not to mention you can get some serious offline traffic if your press release gets picked up by a newspaper. PR Web allows you to distribute a press release to the far corners of the internet, depending on the package you choose.

The important thing to remember when writing the press release is making it newsworthy, so you could technically do a press release for virtually anything that's happening with your website, product, or business. Whenever you launch a new website, for example, you can create a press release and submit it to PR Web. Same goes when you put out a new product.

Although Direct CPV was already briefly mentioned in the CPV section, I never pointed out that you can use their Run of Network (normally referred to as RON) traffic for brand awareness and getting viral marketing campaigns off the ground. Run of Network traffic is untargeted and it runs to all available inventory on the network, so it's an insanely high amount of traffic. You could blow through thousands of dollars very fast, so be careful with it. Don't expect to get any good measurable results with Run of Network traffic on Direct CPV. However, it is possible to use to get thousands of views on a YouTube video in one day, for instance. Just don't expect to use this type of traffic as you would other types.

More Advertising Networks and Ad Sources

- Bravenet Media
- MyAds
- Her Agency
- Indie Click
- Batanga
- 24/7 Media
- BuySellAds
- Adfish
- Crisp Ads
- ExoClick
- Adtegrity
- Intermarkets
- HIRO
- Casale Media
- Banner Space
- Ad On Network
- Advertising.com
- Yahoo Media Services
- AdBuyer.com
- Kitara Media
- Advertise.com
- Flux Advertising
- Burst Media
- Kontera
- Clicksor
- Pepperjam
- TrafficJunky
- Opt-Media
- Mirago
- Miva

- Ad Magnet
- Adblade
- Tribal Fusion
- Pulse360
- Marchex
- PAYPOPUP
- Domain Gateway
- AdMarketplace
- AdEngage
- Chitika
- Traffic Taxi
- Yes Mail
- AdReady
- Bidvertizer
- Zedo
- WeatherBug
- Epic Advertising
- PCH Games
- Popup Traffic
- Bardzo Media
- ADXDirect
- Contextweb
- Adbrite

END OF LESSON 3

If you enjoyed this course, and would like to read my other books on marketing, you can purchase my Kindle book on domain name investing, "Domain flipping Treasure Map" by Kevin Taylor, in paperback, as well as e-book.

With great gratitude,
  Kevin Taylor

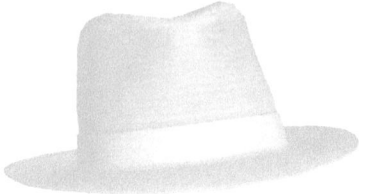

www.ingramcontent.com/pod-product-compliance
Lightning Source LLC
Chambersburg PA
CBHW040235220526
45473CB00001B/252